For the love you've given me through the years... for the sacrifices you made... for the encouragement you gave... for always believing in me... I feel so grateful to have you as my mother. I love you!

ISBN: 978-1-59842-985-5

Children of the Inner Light is a registered trademark. Used under license.

▉ and Blue Mountain Press are registered in U.S. Patent and Trademark Office. Certain trademarks are used under license.

Printed in China.
First Printing: 2016

⊕ This book is printed on recycled paper.

This book is printed on paper that has been specially produced to be acid free (neutral pH) and contains no groundwood or unbleached pulp. It conforms with the requirements of the American National Standards Institute, Inc., so as to ensure that this book will last and be enjoyed by future generations.

Blue Mountain Arts, Inc.
P.O. Box 4549, Boulder, Colorado 80306

To My Mother

A Mother's Love Is a Lasting Treasure

Marci

Blue Mountain Press™
Boulder, Colorado

Mother,
Your Love
Is a
Lasting
Treasure

It takes time and a heart blessed with wisdom to realize the true gift wrapped up in a mother's love. It is easy to take these blessings for granted, because they are given so freely from the day we are born. Today, I want to thank you for all you have given me and let you know how very special you are. You are my mother and my guide, and your love is a lasting treasure.

Our Bond Is Everlasting

I have come to understand and accept that our lives have been brought together for a reason, and for that I am grateful. Your love is what I needed to grow to my fullest potential. I am grateful for the person you are and for your love and caring over the years. You have seen my best and my worst and have loved me. The bond we have found is everlasting.

For All the
Little
Things
You Do...

★

Sometimes I forget to say
"thanks" for all the little things
you do... but I want you to know
that even when I do not say
so, I am so thankful for your
thoughtfulness, your caring,
your willingness to please. Your
efforts never go unnoticed.

★

You Inspire Me!

You have a way of always brightening my day... and it's with little things that mean so much. There is a phone call at just the right time, a hug when it is needed, or a comforting word of encouragement. You are a quiet, steady, burning light that inspires me to be my best.

Your Positive
Spirit Is
Contagious

When my path seems to be filled with roadblocks and I wonder why life is so difficult, you remind me that hope is a gift we can give to ourselves... When we choose this attitude and tap into our inner reserves, we are rewarded with the knowledge of what we have learned in life. The decision to look forward, stay positive, and remain hopeful is a key that unlocks the door to possibilities, and you show me every day the power of hope.

You've Given Me
So Many
Wonderful
Gifts

I ♥ Mom

On the day I was born, I was given a beautiful gift... the gift of having you as my mother. I want you to always remember how thankful I am for this blessing and how much I treasure the priceless things you have given so freely. There is the faith you've shown in me that has allowed me to believe in myself... there is the love you've given me that has taught me to love with all my heart... and there are the values you demonstrated that have given me a foundation for living. These are the gifts that will be with me always.

Thank you
for
Believing
in Me

You are the one who believes in me no matter what... who celebrates my strengths and doesn't seem to notice my weaknesses... who is there for me through thick and thin. I can count on you to be the one who says, "You can do it"... "Hang in there"... and "Everything's going to be okay." I just want you to know how very much this means to me.

You must have had so many dreams for me when I was born, but you let me have my own dreams and supported me through them too.

You watched me grow and change each year, always reminding me to be true to myself in all of life's challenges.

You gave me opportunities that helped me discover who I am and gave me the tools I would need to succeed.

You reminded me so often that I was truly loved, and these times have given me so many precious little moments to save.

You let me go when I am sure you wanted to hold on, and that gave me confidence to find my place in the world.

In so many ways, you have shown me unconditional love.

There Could Never
Be a Better
Mother
Than
You

You are a perfect example of love and caring, compassion and concern. Just talking to you can make me feel better, and being with you reminds me of the most important things in life. Knowing that I have a mother like you is a gift of family and friendship wrapped up in love!

You held me as a baby and let me come into your heart. You nurtured me through childhood and taught me the values that would carry me through life. At times, you let me learn from my own mistakes, but you were always there to dry my tears and share my joys.

You have watched me take my journey and inspired me along the way. You have shared my happiness in everything I do... and you do it all just because you are my mother! I am so glad to have a mother like you.

Home

You're Always There Whenever I Need You

Some days I just need a hand to hold... Some days I just need a hug... Some days I just need a word of encouragement... Some days I just need someone to be there for a laugh and a memory... On my "some days" there is you!

Your Love Is
Never-Ending

Time has brought me a greater understanding of life and a growing appreciation of all you have been to me. As life's plan unfolds and I am gifted with the experience of living, I see you in a new light. I truly know the love you have given and felt over the years, and I am filled with gratitude.

Remember when you sent me off to my first day of school? You had every little detail just right so my beginning would be perfect.

Remember all my birthdays you helped me celebrate? And how you always found a special card?

Remember the hugs of encouragement and the tears you dried along the way?

Remember the worries you had as I was finding my way in the world? And how you "let me go" even though it was hard?

I remember all those things, and as I look back, I feel so loved.

You've Made
Such a
Difference
in My
Life

Mother, I think of you so often and realize just how amazing you are. You have made such a difference in my life. For the many kind words you have spoken, for the thoughtful things you have done, for the way you are always there sharing the special person you are... I am lucky to have a mother like you.

I Love You
and I
Thank
You

There have never been words
more powerful than
"I love you"...
or more meaningful than
"Thank you"...
So I'm saying these things
to you now:
"I love you more
than words can say,
and I thank you
for being a part of my life."

My Wishes
for You...

I hold inside me so many wishes for you... I wish you happiness as you begin each day... special love to warm your heart... and tender memories to store away.

I wish that you have peace in your soul as you begin each day with gratitude.

I wish that you know how much I appreciate the mother you are to me and remember that I love you this day and every day.

I Will Always
Carry Your
Love in
My
Heart

Wherever I go... whatever I do... I will always carry your love in my heart. Your love becomes hope and makes life's challenges bearable. Your love becomes faith and inspires me to do my best. Your love stays in my heart each and every hour of the day and reminds me that I am not alone. I am so glad that I have you in my life.

About Marci

Marci began her career by hand painting floral designs on clothing. No one was more surprised than she was when one day, in a single burst of inspiration and a completely new and different art style, her delightful characters sprang from her pen! "Their wild and crazy hair is a sign of strength," she thought, "and their crooked little smiles are endearing." She quickly identified the charming characters as Mother, Daughter, Sister, Father, Son, Friend, and so on until all the people and places in life were filled. Then, with her own loved ones in mind, she wrote a true and special sentiment to each one. This would be the beginning of a wonderful success story, which today still finds Marci writing each and every one of her verses in this same personal way.

Marci is a self-taught artist who has always enjoyed writing and art. She is thrilled to see how her delightful characters and universal messages of love have touched the hearts and lives of people everywhere. Her distinctive designs can also be found on Blue Mountain Arts greeting cards, calendars, bookmarks, and other gift items.

To learn more about Marci, look for Children of the Inner Light on Facebook or visit her website: www.MARCIonline.com.